PORTFOLIO 1

METROPOLITAN SEMINARS IN ART

Portfolio 1 · *What Is a Painting?*

by John Canaday

CHIEF OF THE DIVISION OF EDUCATION
THE PHILADELPHIA MUSEUM OF ART

THE METROPOLITAN MUSEUM OF ART

INTRODUCTION

WITH this portfolio the Metropolitan Museum presents the first lesson in a systematic course of art study. The plan of the course is original. It is a carefully considered program of art education and of self-education, especially developed by the Museum to help the layman reach some satisfactory understanding of the paintings that attract his interest in the museums of the world, or wherever else he may see them.

The world of art is not a place of mysteries, although it is relatively unfamiliar territory to many of us. A person with enough curiosity could eventually find his way about in it without the guidance that is offered here. With these seminars, however, we hope to smooth his way and speed his passage.

No one is completely innocent in matters of art. The man in the street knows what he likes, or so he is often quoted as saying, even if he may not always be able to tell why. How can he learn to translate his impressions into good judgments? Are there elements that are common to such varied examples as a primitive cave painting, a masterpiece of the High Renaissance, and a canvas by a French impressionist—basic elements that can be made clear and that will serve as helpful guides wherever he may wander in the field of art?

If we can answer these questions satisfactorily, we will have accomplished much. For one thing, we will have relieved to some degree the weariness that afflicts the gallery visitor who perhaps does not really know what he likes or who does not clearly understand why he is supposed to like many of the paintings that hang on museum walls. Visitors who do understand and enjoy what they see in art museums do not tire easily.

We can, of course, get honest delight from a painting without knowing anything about art. But passive acceptance of this pleasure in the presence of a first-rate work of art will not begin to suggest the satisfactions that reward an active and informed approach. These seminars are meant to serve as a practical guide to such an approach. There is no intention here of dictating opinions about what one is *supposed* to like. On the contrary, the aim is to provide information that will enable the reader to develop and fortify his own opinions.

There are no magic formulas that one can apply to arrive at a fixed rating of a painting's quality. The most knowing experts and connoisseurs do not feel quite the same way about any given example. No two people do. And this is as it should be. What we see and enjoy in a painting remains, in the end, a highly personal experience. Indeed, the better we understand the factors that influence our judgment the more strongly we will insist upon this ultimate personal element in appreciation.

Nevertheless, there are many factors beyond pure personal preference that must influence any fair opinion of a painting; and these can be objectively discussed—even reduced to formulas of a sort. It is not possible, for instance, to respond fully to a painting without understanding the means the artist has used to communicate with us, any more than it is possible to grasp the beauty of Shakespeare without first acquiring a vocabulary. Only when the "grammar" of a painting is clearly understood can we begin to interpret it in terms of the artist's intention. The pages that follow this introduction will consider these fundamental factors in detail and in orderly sequence.

It may be seriously questioned whether there

has been any measurable improvement in man's ability to express himself artistically during the last several thousand years. There have been changes galore in the style and manner of such expressions, to be sure. But where is the bold man who would claim, much less who could prove, that a drawing by Picasso or Matisse more cogently and expressively reveals the human spirit than the prehistoric drawings in the caves of Lascaux or Altamira?

THE art of the painter at its best is a revelation of truth as well as the artist could state it. Like truth told in any other medium, the painter's truth has its degrees and its fortunes. Like musical compositions and poems or novels, the works of some painters have soared for a time in public esteem and then fizzled like burned-out rockets. The works of others have been ignored or neglected for a period and then have risen to a level of lasting brightness. Our grandfathers, for example, were unaware of El Greco. Their grandfathers celebrated some painters we will never hear of again.

Yet painting, like the other arts, seems to be subject to a kind of natural selection in time. Someone has remarked that art is whatever has been considered art for the longest time by the most people who are supposed to know. In spite of the occasional startling rediscoveries of neglected artists and the occasional shaking down of some reputations, there is, on the part of those who are "supposed to know," as much or more common agreement here as we are likely to find in the field of philosophy or history, for example.

THESE seminars will explain the explainable and leave the reader in a position to reach the ultimate conclusions on his own terms. He will be in a far stronger position than his grandfather was. Modern techniques of color photoengraving, such as are used to produce the plates in this portfolio, make it possible for layman and scholar alike to form valid impressions of works of art that are scattered about the globe, works which would have remained beyond the reach of any but the most determined and fortunate traveler a generation or two ago. This relatively new development is one of those luxuries of our age which, like television and the airplane, have already become commonplace.

What follows, then, will be neither a history of art nor a discussion of isolated masterpieces. It will, on the other hand, reproduce and consider broad cross sections of significant paintings of all the ages, relating them to separate principles of criticism. The farther we go, the more we will see that the enjoyment of painting is a cumulative experience. Nothing is ever lost. Discovery becomes easier and richer from painting to painting. The reader should find that the impetus given by these seminars will carry far beyond the limits of our course. For, to paraphrase the author, every painting that is enjoyed through clear understanding will increase our enjoyment and understanding of all other paintings.

MARSHALL B. DAVIDSON
Editor of Publications
The Metropolitan Museum of Art

WHAT IS A PAINTING?

A PAINTING is a layer of pigments applied to a surface. It is an arrangement of shapes and colors. It is a projection of the personality of the man who painted it, a statement of the philosophy of the age that produced it, and it can have a meaning beyond anything concerned with one man or only one period of time.

But most people see a painting first of all as a picture. It is a picture *of* something—a pretty woman, a landscape, a seascape or a cityscape, a bowl of fruit, a meadow with cows. And beyond the subject of the picture the average person sees very little. He looks at a painting and sees a man, or a dog, a vase of flowers, the Madonna, a battlefield, a small boy stealing cookies, and that is that.

To judge the merits of a painting by this standard is a simple affair. The picture is good first to the extent that the objects represented in it "look real" and second to the extent that the subject conforms to established ideas of what is entertaining (the small boy stealing cookies) or beautiful (the vase of flowers) or uplifting (the Madonna) or simply informative.

For this point of view there is something to be said, but not much. Forgetting modern abstract art for the moment we will admit that *all* painting does *begin* with a subject. But the subject should be only a point of departure.

Take, as an instance, the picture universally but incorrectly known as Whistler's Mother (Plate 1). It comes off very well by the standards we have just mentioned. It "looks real" to such a degree that it suggests soft-focus photography *(Figure 1)*. And its subject immediately calls into play the double reverence we feel for motherhood and old age. These associations are stirred up even more vigorously because this picture of a mother in her old age was painted by her own son, adding filial devotion to the already impressive sum of human virtue tied in with the subject. With such admirable connections Whistler's Mother might have found its way into popular favor even if it had been a very bad picture. It happens to be a very fine picture but *not* because it is a lifelike portrait of an old lady by her son.

The correct title of this picture is still the one Whistler originally gave it and always insisted upon: Arrangement in Gray and Black. And its real subject is a mood, a mood compounded of gentleness, dignity, reflection, and resignation. This mood may be suggested by the subject, but it is completed by the shapes and colors Whistler chooses to use and the relationship he establishes among them. This is called *composition,* and it is the most important single factor in the expressive quality of a painting.

Now it is obvious that the quiet and tender mood Whistler had in mind could not be relayed to the observer through vivid colors and jagged shapes in complex or agitated relationship to one another. Hence the artist reduces the background to a few subtly spaced rectangles of subdued neutral tones, and against this background the figure of the old lady is reduced to a silhouette nearly as geometrical and just as uneventful. The head, the hands, and the scattering of luminous flecks on the curtain serve as relieving accents, lighter in tone and livelier in shape, in a scheme that might otherwise have been monotonous and melancholy.

We said a moment ago that even if this had been a bad picture it might have been a popular one. But it would never have become so widely known and loved as it is now, because even the average person who never doubts that his enjoyment comes from the subject matter of Whistler's Mother is being affected, even if he doesn't realize it, by the expressive composition of Arrangement in Gray and Black.

Composition affects our reaction to a picture whether or not we think of it in compositional terms. If the composition is successful we respond as the artist intended us to, without asking ourselves why. But once we are aware of composition as an element in painting we have the additional pleasure of discovering how the artist goes about evoking the response he is after. These two pleasures are perfectly compatible. In the same way, we may be moved by a great performance in the theater while simultaneously, quite aside from our emotional participation, we admire the actor's skill.

The structure of a composition can be tested by framing off different areas with pieces of paper. Effective little pictures-within-pictures may be isolated in this way, but the fragments can never say the same thing as the total of a good composition, not because part of the subject matter is eliminated but because the relationship of the shapes and colors has been disturbed. If everything in Arrangement in Gray and Black is blocked off except the central figure you still have a picture of an old lady sitting in a chair. Nothing has been eliminated that tells part of a story or adds to what we know about this particular woman. But the picture's mood is gone. This picture, in fact, suffers in countless cheap reproductions where it is chopped off along the edges for convenience in putting into a frame or onto a page.

Subject and No Subject

Since Whistler insisted on calling the painting Arrangement in Gray and Black and since we have just been arguing that the composition carries the statement of mood, we may ask whether this picture would be just as affecting if we omitted the subject altogether. It would not be difficult to put a dark cape and a couple of pale objects of some kind on the chair, thus reproducing the missing silhouettes if the figure of the old lady were taken out. Would we be losing anything?

A few years ago this would have been a facetious proposition, but today the question comes up seriously. The abstract school of contemporary painters argues that subject matter is only something that gets in the way. It confuses the issue—the issue being pure expression by means of color, texture, line, and shape existing in their own right and representing nothing at all. Abstract painting, which may get so abstract that the "picture" is reduced to a few neat rectangles of color and a few neat black lines neatly disposed upon the canvas, is the artist's final release from the associative emotional values Whistler tried to avoid when he gave his mother's portrait the title he did. Whether the abstract painter gains more than he is losing is a question that must be discussed in a later portfolio. In the meantime we will assume that the subject of a painting *is* important because it is a source of meaning. But what we must remember is that the true meaning may be some distance removed from the apparent subject.

In short, painting is interpretation, not imitation; a painting is great to the extent that it enlarges our experience, to the extent that it enriches or clarifies our inner world—*not* to the extent that it echoes the look of the world around us.

Four Women: Madame Leblanc

Whistler's portrait of his mother is especially clear in demonstrating the point that a painting is an expressive arrangement of shapes and colors. But we also contended that a painting is "a projection of the personality of the man who painted it, and a statement of the philosophy of the age that produced it." These points also could be made with reference to Arrangement in Gray and Black but less explicitly. We will illustrate them instead by comparing four other pictures, all of them portraits of young women, all

Figure 1

9

Figure 2

of them fine or even great pictures, none of them alike.

Ingres's Madame Leblanc (Plate 2) is more easily understood than the others because its intention is less profound. It has, superbly, what most of us want in a woman's portrait—attractive grace, impeccable technique, and a personable sitter. It tells us nothing more about Madame Leblanc than that she was a member of the prosperous upper middle class endowed with a certain pleasant combination of features.

Since it is the work of the most eminent portraitist of his day, we may take for granted that the likeness of Madame Leblanc has the required combination of veracity and flattery that a photographer achieves today by retouching. Madame Leblanc's features were probably less regular than they are shown here *(Figure 2),* her neck less elegant, and her fingers not so beautifully tapered *(Figure 3).* Without question, Ingres has made the most of her good points and minimized her shortcomings. The lady is further beautified by the presence of the exquisitely painted shawl, the jewelry, and the suggestions of fashionable interior decoration, since in a picture all

the elements partake of the quality of all the others.

Madame Leblanc's is an utterly charming portrait. Perhaps it can suggest, too, the way of life of a certain class of people during a certain period in France, if we are already familiar with that period, but as an *interpretation,* as an effort to present anything more than an entrancing effigy, it hardly exists, for it makes no attempt to explore the personality of the sitter.

This is, of course, a legitimate approach even if it is a limited one. The picture has a virtue imperative to all good painting—harmony between what the painter wants to do and the means he uses to do it. Elegance, grace, and refinement disciplined by exquisite drawing and patterned by an artist with a genius for the creation of beautiful line—this is the recipe for an Ingres portrait. Further study could reveal complications and nuances, but essentially this is a picture we can accept at its most apparent values. It is all it appears to be—not much more, nothing less. Compositionally the painting is a suave disposition of shapes whose contours have been designed into linear delights, and while this may have a great deal to do with the fact that this particular effigy is entrancing, it is not exactly an interpretation of the subject since Ingres applied the same formula to virtually every subject he painted.

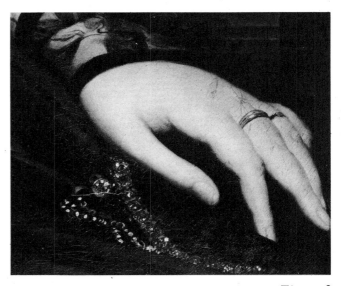

Figure 3

10

Madame Renoir

But not every picture, not even every portrait of a woman, wants to be or say the same thing. Madame Leblanc must have been delighted with her portrait. She would certainly have been offended if she had been painted as Renoir painted his wife (Plate 3).

Unlike Madame Leblanc's, this portrait holds deeper meanings beneath the simplicity of its apparent subject. This simplicity is extreme. A round-faced and buxom young woman in a hat and blouse sits facing us, smiling, her hands resting in her lap. That is all. There is no background of landscape, nor of a room, not even of drapery. The entire image is there for us at a glance, without elaboration or distractions. Its appeal is immediate. It is bright, fresh, and happy.

Still, any number of pictures of young women are bright, fresh, and happy but are not in museums. What makes this one so important that its value, expressed materially, is tens of thousands of dollars? What does it have that any bright, fresh, happy magazine cover does not? What makes Renoir a great painter?

He was a fine technician, but so were hundreds of other painters of his generation who could do anything they wanted with a brush except paint great pictures. He had a great talent, but he was not a genius. His life, as a series of events, holds nothing extraordinary. He lived through early struggles to see himself accepted at last as an important artist, but so did many of his contemporaries whose names have been forgotten, whose pictures now seem so dull and pretentious that they have been relegated in quantity to museum basements.

It is as simple as this: Renoir is a great painter because he had a joyous adoration of life and the ability to translate it into visual terms so that all of us may understand and share it. Other fortunate men have held the same joyous faith. No other painter has combined it with Renoir's special gift to express it so richly for the rest of us. Other painters are great for entirely different reasons. This particular greatness is Renoir's own.

His art flows from an unwavering conviction of the world's goodness. He sees happiness, in its deepest sense, as the natural state of mankind. He finds it everywhere in the world around him. His art is direct, simple, and profound because it reflects a personal philosophy which is direct, simple, and profound. For Renoir, life is such a miracle that simply to take part in it gives meaning to existence.

His In the Meadow (Plate 4)—we will return to the portrait of his wife in a moment—sums up his joyousness in an especially fresh and delicious painting. The canvas shimmers with color. Everything glows with budding fertility. The grass, the trees, the landscape in the distance, the young girls, even the light and air that permeate the picture—everything blossoms and breathes in the perfection of a spring day. There is nothing unusual about the girls or the meadow where they sit. Renoir's subjects are never unusual. He paints in the conviction that the greatest values in life are, quite naturally, the simplest ones.

For Renoir these values are materialized and concentrated in woman—but not woman as a temptress, not even as an individual, and certainly not as a being with psychological quirks and fancies worth exploring. She is none of these things because she is something more: she is the source of all warmth and life in the world. Children, flowers, and fruit are natural adjuncts of this conception. Renoir's men, when they appear at all, appear as suitors, not with the aggressive force of the conquering male but as gentle idolators of the female principle. It is this conception of woman as a basic universal symbol that makes the difference between the importance of a Renoir painting and the triviality of a merely attractive magazine cover no matter how skillfully the magazine cover may be executed and no matter how successfully it fulfills its limited function.

And so, returning to the portrait of Madame Renoir, the picture has a second and deeper meaning beneath its apparent one. It becomes the image of an earth goddess, while it remains

Figure 4

the tender record of an unexceptional young woman in a straw hat with a couple of roses pinned to it. In other words, the picture's message is universal, expressed in terms of the particular, a recipe for the interpretation of the world which in one variation or another has been effective for more than two thousand years and remains as vigorous as ever.

How does Renoir go about creating this universal symbol?

First, by using his subject as it existed in nature only as a point of departure and by modifying it to suggest the eternal quality that woman, for him, represents. Artists of all periods, when they hunt a meaning beneath the transient surfaces of things, begin to think in terms of geometric design. The fundamental nature of a symbol is somehow harmonious with the finality of a simple geometrical form.

Try now to see the portrait of Madame Renoir not as a picture of a young woman but as a structure of strong, solid volumes.

These volumes, these forms, are much simpler than a literal reproduction of the model's appearance would have been. As Renoir has drawn them, the face and the crown of the hat describe a solid, regular oval *(Figure 4)*. It is no accident that in the hat brim he repeats his first oval in the opposite direction. And the mass of the figure, if we follow a line along the shoulders and arms, approximates half an oval of the same shape, although it is larger and slightly irregular. The neck is a cylinder, and this same sturdy form is repeated, although not quite so obviously, in the arms.

If such an analysis sounds artificial it is because the total effect of a work of art is more than the sum of the technical means used to achieve it. The point is that Renoir reduces his subject to large, solid, uncomplicated masses because such forms are suggestive of eternal values.

The danger Renoir runs in modifying the image in this direction is that it may become ponderous and inert. Hence he throws the figure slightly off balance (toward our right). As a kind of grace note, to relieve and accentuate the stability of the main forms, he combines the little bouquet of leaves and roses into a more broken silhouette, although he allows it at the same time to echo the oval forms. Finally he gives full freedom to the curling irregularities of the escaping locks of hair. The sharp V's in the lapels and the neckline of the blouse serve as contrast to the dominating rounded forms. The more we study the painting in this way the more we see that everything in this deceptively simple composition is planned and that to change any of it, for instance to make the button much larger or smaller, to change its position, or make it one of a row of buttons would put this detail out of its most harmonious relationship to the rest of the picture.

The image combines a sense of vivid life with its stability. Much of this life comes from the rich sparkle of the pigment. The picture would be ruinously transformed if it were repainted with the almost chilly precision which is appropriate to the Madame Leblanc or with the softness of a Whistler. It is difficult to say why Renoir's paint is so alive. It is a matter of "touch" —the despair of the analytical critic, the defeat of the forger, the birthright of the natural painter, and for the observer a direct source of communication with the artist.

As for its reflection of a time and a place, the picture is French through and through. Mystical or near-mystical veneration of woman is a constant factor in French art, expressed in forms ranging from medieval statues of the Virgin to allegorical portraits of eighteenth-century courtesans. At the core of French life, too, there is a love and respect for simple things. Renoir is directly in line with both of these traditions at once, but he expresses them in terms of his own century. The nineteenth century placed its faith neither in medieval mysteries nor in eighteenth-century refinements. Its true faith was in the commonplace. So is Renoir's. But he lifts the commonplace into the realm of the ideal and performs the additional feat of doing so without loss of intimacy.

Woman with Chrysanthemums

In discussing the Renoir as if it had achieved a kind of perfection, as indeed it has, it may seem that we have left nothing for other portraits of women to achieve. But the glory of the art of painting is that it offers no single perfection but a multitude of perfections. We will compare the Renoir to a picture by his friend and close contemporary, Edgar Degas, whose Woman with Chrysanthemums (Plate 5) was painted within a few miles and a few years of the Renoir.

We can imagine what Renoir would have done with the subject. Woman and flowers would have fused into a glowing symbol of bountiful fruition. But such an interpretation was impossible for Degas; he was as doubtful of life's goodness as Renoir was certain of it.

Degas's art reveals a man who is essentially a pessimist. He is not certain that he knows the meaning of life, not even certain that one exists. He is a doubter, except on one score: of life's fascination as a continuous, if haphazard, spectacle he holds no doubt whatsoever. He is absorbed by the look of people, especially women, as they go about their daily affairs. He might be described as a passionate spectator. He is sensitive to human beings as psychological phenomena rather than (as Renoir's women must have seemed to him) as masses of protoplasm.

Like Renoir, Degas is a nineteenth-century Frenchman preoccupied with woman and the commonplace. But he is not the same kind of man as Renoir, and he is going to reflect this subject matter in a contrasting way.

Woman with Chrysanthemums is a brilliantly eccentric composition. Ordinarily the subject of a portrait holds the center of the canvas. Degas pushes this one far to one side. Ordinarily the subject either looks directly at the observer or regards some object within the frame or, at most, looks dreamily into space. This one looks out beyond the picture at something apparently familiar to her but unidentified and tantalizingly unidentifiable to us *(Figure 5)*. The average portrait builds up its brightest colors and strongest contrasts in ways which insure the subject its rightful climax of interest. But Degas not only gives over the center of this picture to a brilliant explosion of flowers while he crowds his subject against the frame; he also paints the woman in virtual monochrome and allows her to conceal part of her face with one hand. By violating all the conventions of portrait composition Degas achieves a picture brilliant beyond anything most painters achieve by following them.

Why does he compose in this eccentric way? Because where Renoir composed to create an expression of eternal stability, Degas wants us to feel that we have come upon the woman with the chrysanthemums by chance. Where Renoir is enraptured by life in its wholeness, Degas is fascinated by its fragments. He composed the majority of his pictures, like this one, as if they were segments of larger compositions. Paradoxically, though, this chance effect is meticulously controlled. Degas never falls into the trap of novelty for its own sake. His compositions are always as sound as they are original, as satisfying as they are provocative.

We saw Renoir rejecting background in the portrait of his wife to increase the universality of the image. A specific background tends to define place and time, thus reducing the timelessness and everywhereness appropriate to a universal symbol. Naturally Degas, interested in life as a transient spectacle, sharply defines the locale and the moment. In Woman with Chrysanthemums we can deduce such specific factors as the social level and financial bracket of the subject just as we could with Madame Leblanc. But we are also aware of the Woman with Chrysanthemums as a person capable of thinking and acting in certain ways under certain circumstances.

But in the end she remains enigmatic, as Degas surely intended her to do. She half hides a half-smile, which may be half mocking. In her feminine elusiveness she is like another woman, known to us all in the most famous portrait in the world, painted about four centuries earlier: Degas's Woman with Chrysanthemums is a nineteenth-century Mona Lisa.

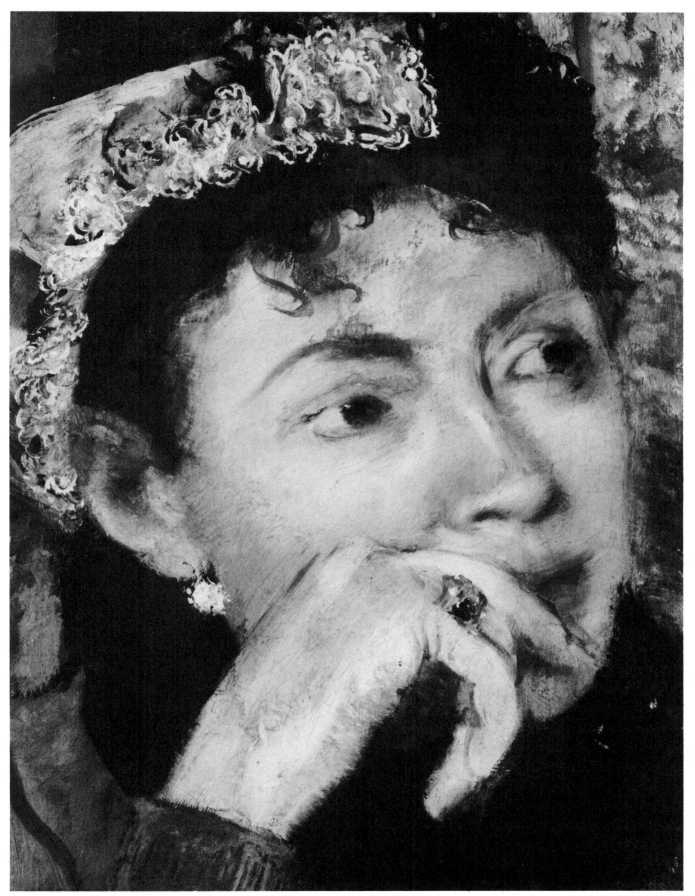

Figure 5

15

Mona Lisa

Leonardo da Vinci's Mona Lisa (Plate 6), like the Renoir and the Degas we have just seen, is only secondarily a representation of the sitter, whose identity has been the subject of a great deal of speculation. But the actual sitter, if there was one, is of no importance. The Mona Lisa is a personality created by Leonardo da Vinci.

It is a bizarre picture. Some of its bizarre features have been made bizarre by time. The eyebrows are shaved, and the hairline is raised far back by plucking or shaving in accord with a fashion of the day. The costume, richly theatrical to us, may also have been modish. But these are minor considerations. The serious difficulty anyone must meet in understanding the Mona Lisa is that it has been too famous for too long. Familiar legends and conjectures have accumulated around it to the point where it is impossible to see it with a fresh vision. We never see it for the first time; it has always been around. It is no longer a picture; it is an institution.

The most irritating legend attached to the Mona Lisa is that the eyes "follow you around the room" through some secret way of painting known only to Leonardo and unique to this picture. The eyes of any portrait where the subject looks directly at the observer appear to follow him, no matter how ineptly they are executed. Then there is the superstition that the lips, if stared at long enough, "begin to smile." Any object stared at to the point of strain will appear to change in one way or another, especially if we expect it to. It is unfortunate, also, that the Mona Lisa is so often called the greatest picture in the world. No picture can be the greatest in the world, because there is no single standard of perfection. If such a standard could exist, it is difficult to see how so ambiguous a picture as the Mona Lisa could represent it anyway.

Such difficulties explain why efforts to interpret the painting have a way of degenerating into literary maunderings like Walter Pater's notorious one, which has become the standard example of what art criticism is not:

She is older than the rocks among which she sits; like the vampire, she has been dead many times, and learned the secrets of the grave; and has been a diver in deep seas, and keeps their fallen days about her; and trafficked for strange webs with Eastern merchants, and, as Leda, was the mother of Helen of Troy, and, as Saint Anne, the mother of Mary; and all this has been to her but as the sound of lyres and flutes, and lives only in the delicacy with which it has moulded the changing lineaments, and tinged the eyelids and the hands.

Be that as it may, our concern is with the similarities and differences, four centuries removed, between the Mona Lisa and the Woman with Chrysanthemums as examples of the way pictures reflect the time and place of their creation.

Degas's picture would have been inconceivable to a man of the Italian Renaissance. It would have been intellectual heresy to suggest to Leonardo that a painting like Woman with Chrysanthemums, deliberately emphasizing the transient, the casual, and the everyday, could be just as effective in suggesting woman's enigmatic quality as the Mona Lisa with all its idealization. Renaissance man sought an ideal, and this ideal was *order*. Leonardo was as fascinated by the world as Degas was, but being a renaissance man he refused to accept its accidents, its imperfections, its confusion, and its discord. The Mona Lisa is purified of all suggestion of the temporary, the haphazard, or the commonplace. The picture exists with such calm that Woman with Chrysanthemums, alongside, seems vivacious; and it is so impervious to the moment that the Degas becomes by comparison a comment on life's evanescence.

Oddly enough, it is possible to make some fairly direct parallels between the portrait of Madame Renoir and the Mona Lisa. What we have said about the oval of the head in the Renoir, the cylinder of the neck and arms, the mass of the rest of the figure, is applicable to the forms in the Mona Lisa too. But instead of Renoir's vigorous image we have a subtle, almost sly, even morbid one. Correspondingly, the forms in the Renoir face us directly. They are straightforward, while those in the Mona Lisa shift and turn. Leonardo presents us with the face from one angle, turns the body at another, shifts the arms to yet a third in order to return the curious, boneless hands *(Figure 6)* to the same frontal position as the face.

logical, where both time and place are mysterious. Mona Lisa's head, played against this background, partakes of its qualities, just as Madame Leblanc shared the fashionable elegance of the various accessories to her portrait.

Madame Leblanc, Madame Renoir, the

Figure 6

If Leonardo intended to make the Mona Lisa a symbol of timeless mysteries, the landscape in the background plays a major part in this expression. True, this seems to contradict what we have just said in connection with the Renoir and the Degas about backgrounds reducing universality by defining time and place. But Leonardo has invented a landscape half fantastic and half

Woman with Chrysanthemums, and Mona Lisa. Ingres could have made any one of these women into a lovely effigy; Renoir, any one of them into an earth goddess; Degas, any one of them into a complete individual within a fragmented world; Leonardo, any one of them into an idealized enigma. The subject of a picture is only a point of departure for whatever the painter has to say.

17

Thinking, Feeling, and Painting

Once we have passed beyond the barrier of pure subject, our enjoyment of painting is limited only by our capacity to respond emotionally and intellectually to the infinitely varied expressions of the human spirit offered us in the art of all times and all places. This enjoyment is sometimes weighted on the side of thinking, sometimes on the side of feeling, and the artist works under the same double stimulus.

There is a popular and absurd conception of the "inspired" artist who works in a kind of hypnotic frenzy. His creations gush forth from some hidden reservoir of emotion without any effort on his part, although sometimes with considerable physical agitation followed by dramatic exhaustion. This simply does not happen. Or if it does happen, what gushes forth is formless and chaotic and hence not art.

At the opposite pole are the few painters who have tried to eliminate all emotional and intuitive factors in an effort to work by pure calculation, even by mathematical formulas. This is absurd too, since even the most intellectualized painting must tie somewhere to the world of feeling, just as the most emotionalized must depend to some extent upon disciplined knowledge.

The words "romantic" and "classic" have so many meanings that we must define the way we will use them here: "romantic" will designate paintings making their first appeal to the emotions or imagination no matter how much calculation is involved; "classic" will refer to those

Figure 7

18

making their strongest appeal to the intellect no matter what emotional implications are present. We will look at two paintings similar in subject, one treated romantically and the other classically. Either one is crippled if we try to force it into the other's category. The important thing to remember is that we limit our enjoyment of painting if we don't allow a tolerance for both points of view, no matter which of them appeals to us first by nature. Romantic painting is diffuse and exaggerated by the standards of classical discipline. Classicism turns frigid if we expect romantic emotionalism of it.

The romantic painting, Durand's Imaginary Landscape (Plate 7), has a quicker general appeal than Cézanne's Mont Sainte-Victoire (Plate 8), since most people look at landscape romantically, particularly in England and America where we are conditioned by the English poets to see landscape as they saw it. Also, Imaginary Landscape is painted in a good, sound, conventional manner reassuring to the lay observer. With the more knowing this manner is just now out of fashion, and they will pass by Durand for Cézanne. This is a mistake. Both paintings are first-rate achievements of different intentions.

Durand painted in America in the middle of the nineteenth century when romantic glorification of nature was most popular. The painters of his school were fond of grandiose panoramas receding into infinite space, of shadowy foregrounds or valleys filled with crags rising into dramatic lights. The majestic towering of trees, clouds, and mountains was set off by such intimate detail as grazing sheep, men on horseback, people going about their little work. Ruined architecture on rocky peaks or small habitations in sheltering crannies suggested the infiltration of man into nature's vastness but remained diminutive or even spectral in the magnitude of their setting *(Figure 7)*.

In his Imaginary Landscape Durand is free to assemble all these trappings unfettered by the necessity of approximating the look of any actual scene, and the painting becomes a kind of summary of all the devices he and his fellow painters

Figure 8

employed to invest nature with an air of mysterious grandeur. His imaginary mountains recede in ranges of pinnacles; a river stretches into the distance to culminate in the drama of the sun, hovering in space and illuminating the whole complicated spectacle by its colored light. Detail by detail the picture is explicit *(Figure 8),* but it does not seek so much to capture an illusion of nature as it does to intensify the awesome sensations we would feel if we could be confronted by the landscape itself.

Romantic landscape was nothing new. There is hardly a device in Durand's picture that had not already been worn threadbare in European painting. But Durand uses them with all the enthusiasm of a discoverer. The reappearance of a whole school of romantic landscape artists in the United States in the mid-nineteenth century (Imaginary Landscape was painted in 1850) is at least partially explained by America's sense of excitement as the incredible reaches of our West and Northwest began to open up. Today this excitement is tempered by ease of travel and over-familiarity through photography, especially through motion pictures. We can be all the more thankful that we have paintings recording for us the sense of mystery and wildness and greatness which has so diminished during the past hundred years.

19

Romantic Mystery and Classical Order

But mystery and wildness are exactly the opposite of the qualities Cézanne sought, and achieved, in his Mont Sainte-Victoire. Faced by the Rocky Mountains, this good Frenchman would simply have been appalled at the prospect of putting them into order. Nature's romantic mystery does not interest him; he is interested only in revealing its underlying clarity and logic.

In Mont Sainte-Victoire the sky is a curtain bounding the limits of the picture rather than an opening into infinite depth where the eye and the imagination are led. We do not wander away or escape from the Cézanne; we remain within its established boundaries. Cézanne's mountain exists as one large, tangible, firmly integrated mass; Durand's mountains are complicated in form, they vanish here and there into suggestive shadowy recesses, or rise from them unexpectedly. The world within Cézanne's frame reaches us at first glance in its entirety; we discover Durand's bit by bit as we explore it, led from detail to detail. Cézanne means his landscape to be complete. Durand means his to be inexhaustible.

Cézanne's subject happens to be an actual place, but he does not reproduce it. And if Durand could have sat beside Cézanne to paint the same scene, he would have found material for a landscape as romantic as Cézanne's is classic, as open as Cézanne's is self-contained. Nature in itself is meaningless; it is only as we interpret it that it has meaning. Durand seeks to open his landscape to the infinite reaches of the imagination. Cézanne seeks to contract his within the comprehension of the intellect. Through the two pictures we may respond to both points of view.

We must admit at this point that Cézanne's art is difficult for the beginner. He was a revolutionary as far as technique is concerned, and his quality of order may not be apparent at first glance. Nor will it ever become apparent if the picture is regarded as an effort to imitate the appearance of nature. There is intentionally very little expression of depth. The space is kept shallow, and the picture generally is highly abstract —that is, the forms in it tend to lose their identity as real objects and exist for form's sake. This, too, is the opposite of the Durand, where every form is recognizable in detail and surrounded by a host of associations.

If you can sense that Durand regards nature as a manifestation of mysterious forces while Cézanne regards it as an expression of the essential orderliness upon which the world must depend for its meaning, then you have understood the basic contrast between the two pictures and the two points of view, romantic and classic.

Special Problems in Special Pictures

We have been talking so far as if certain general principles, once understood, can make all painting understandable. Fortunately this is more true than not, but some pictures carry their message in disguises that must be penetrated individually.

Figure 9

20

The disguise in Edward Hicks's The Peaceable Kingdom (Plate 9) is no puzzle to anyone who

Figure 10

has a nodding acquaintance with American colonial history and the Old Testament. In the foreground a congregation of animals and children illustrates three verses from the eleventh chapter of Isaiah *(Figure 9):*

> The wolf also shall dwell with the lamb, and the leopard shall lie down with the kid; and the calf and the young lion and the fatling together; and a little child shall lead them.
> And the cow and the bear shall feed; their young ones shall lie down together: and the lion shall eat straw like the ox.
> And the sucking child shall play on the hole of the asp, and the weaned child shall put his hand on the cockatrice' den.

The good American Quaker preacher who painted The Peaceable Kingdom has followed these verses to the letter. Like other self-taught painters he cultivates a meticulous technique. Unlike most of them he is an inventive designer. He is an artist. If he does not always draw as well as he wishes he could, he never fails as a creator of patterns. The lack of conventional skills accentuates the innate artistry of the man and ac-

counts for the arresting quaintness of his work.

So far the picture is only a biblical illustration invested with an agreeable air of fantasy by the painter's individual style. But in the background is a second illustration, William Penn concluding his treaty with the Indians *(Figure 10)*. The picture now becomes a political or even sociological allegory. The peaceable kingdom of the Bible is reflected on earth through the concord of the red man and the white man, and the Quaker preacher has left for us a confident statement of his belief that peace on earth and good will toward men is a realizable ideal.

It would be foolish to pretend that The Peaceable Kingdom rises to great expressive heights. It has charm rather than power; it is pious rather than profound, touching rather than moving. But it does enlarge our experience, as we have said painting should do, by admitting us to a world of gentle faith which is no less true for being so small and so far away.

Meaning through Symbols

If we were ignorant of its historical and biblical references, The Peaceable Kingdom would be only a curious representation of animals, children, and men conducting themselves implausibly in a landscape. In this same way virtually everybody misses the significance of Jan van Eyck's double portrait of Giovanni Arnolfini and his wife, Giovanna Cenami (Plate 10). Probably not one person in a thousand among the tens of thousands who stop in front of it where it hangs in London's National Gallery suspects that its details are anything more than fascinating curiosities.

Even so, it is one of the most compelling pictures in the world. This grave, beautifully costumed couple are such convincing personalities that once we have met them they persist in our memory as real people. We remember their air of consequence and solemnity, although it is odd that they should be pictured thus, standing in a bedroom and surrounded by trivia: a little dog *(Figure 11)*, pieces of fruit scattered on the window sill, and a pair of pattens discarded on the floor. It is odd that there is only one candle in the chandelier, odd too that it is burning in the daytime, and that the artist has inscribed his name so conspicuously on the back wall *(Figure 12)*. This last is additionally surprising since at the time the picture was painted, more than five hundred years ago, it was unusual for a painter to sign his work at all.

The fact is that as we stand before this picture we are witnesses at a marriage ceremony. The air of solemnity is explained when we know that the hands are joined in the marriage oath. The painter is not only painter but witness and has inscribed his name on the wall in legal script of the kind proper to a document. And the picture *is* a document in effect—a marriage certificate. These two fine and serious people first solemnized their own marriage in complete solitude, as was possible under canon law at that time. Later the picture was commissioned to reaffirm and record the event, and the "trivia" are not trivia at all but symbolic references to the sacramental nature of the scene before us.

The discarded pattens *(Figure 13)* refer to the biblical command, "Put off thy shoes from off thy feet, for the place whereon thou standest is holy ground." This same symbol is used in other pictures, notably Crucifixions, to establish the holy or sacramental nature of the spot, which in this case is the nuptial chamber. The dog symbolizes the marital virtue of faithfulness, the fruit refers to the fruit of the Garden of Eden, and the single candle is a multiple symbol. It combines overlapping references to the candle that was carried in wedding processions and the burning candle frequently required at the taking of an oath, which is also the candle as a symbol of the all-seeing eye of God.

The mirror on the wall symbolizes purity. The

Figure 11

Figure 12

23

carved figure on the chair near the bed is Saint Margaret, the patron saint of childbirth. All of these symbols were standard ones, now half forgotten but familiar five hundred years ago, and their combination within a single picture is too consistent to be coincidental. Their rediscovery in relationship to the subjects of this double portrait (see the Notes on the Painters at the end of this portfolio) changed it from one of the most intriguing pictures ever painted into one of the most impressive pictures in the world.

Figure 13

Good Art, Bad Art, and Modern Art

No general discussion of painting should conclude without some consideration of modern art, which means the question of the way ideas change as to what is good art and what is bad art. We will compare two paintings as representative combatants in the pitched battle between modernism and traditional academic painting that has been going on in a mild way forever but with great violence for the past hundred years. While the battle continues, we will select an area where the dust has settled.

Pierre Cot's The Storm (Plate 11), painted in 1880, representing the losers, was a tremendously popular picture once but has now dropped to the nadir of critical esteem. A similar picture sent to the jury of any major exhibition today would be laughed out of the gallery. Kokoschka's The Tempest (Plate 12) has an opposite history. It was painted in 1914 when Kokoschka's art was still damned as degenerate by a public, and by most critics, who could still stretch a point backward to admire pictures like the Cot. Today the Kokoschka cannot look very radical to anybody, and even the uninitiated layman would hesitate to damn it although he might be unable to respond with full sympathy. We will discuss it first.

There is no actual "tempest" visible. We see a pair of lovers encompassed by forms like windy clouds or waves or a nightmarish landscape. The color, dominated by turgid blues and greens, suggests (but does not represent) a stormy sky shot through here and there with light. These swirling colors surround the figures of a watchful man and a sleeping woman who are intertwined not only with one another but with the surrounding swirls of color as well. They are not handsome people. Their bodies are twisted, deformed, and discolored. Yet they are serene in the midst of all the surrounding violence. Whether or not the painter thought of his subject in exactly these terms, the picture says that human love is the sustaining miracle of goodness in the confusion and malevolence of life. The figures are "ugly" because they must participate in life; they are worn by it. They have not escaped from life, they have found a refuge within it.

The theme is an affecting one but could easily turn mawkish. Kokoschka expresses it with a vigor that would be weakened if his lovers were glamorous creatures immune to hardship or ill fortune and the normal difficulties of existence.

Such an unreal and idyllic immunity is suggested by the pretty lovers who flee the storm in Cot's painting. Like Kokoschka's, they are beset by the elements. Both painters express the oneness of the lovers by tying them together with interlacing lines and a billowing, surrounding form (in the Cot, the wind-filled drapery). Both

trait of Madame Renoir became one when we stopped regarding it as the portrait of a particular woman.

Compared with the strength of the Kokoschka, Cot's picture seems today a flossy bit of picture-making concerned with second-rate values. It is a

Figure 14

suggest the relationship of protective male to more fragile female. But beneath these similarities the differences are extreme.

An important one is that the Cot is specific and detailed in such a way that it becomes an illustration of the plight of one particular pair of lovers, while the Kokoschka is generalized and abstracted. In a more emotionalized way the Kokoschka is a universal image just as the por-

wondrously slick piece of work, but nothing much goes on beneath this surface of technical display. For all the signposts such as billowing drapery and bodily attitudes pointing out that the figures are supposed to be running, there is no expression of flight. The lovers remain frozen forever on tiptoe *(Figure 14)* continuing to suggest models posing in the studio. Kokoschka's figures are integrated with the rest of the picture, but Cot's stand in front of a photographer's backdrop. Our attention is constantly urged toward their prettiness, not toward their quality as human beings, and we are asked to admire the rendition of such incidentals as the horn at the boy's belt, the girl's filmy gown, and all the unnecessary complexities of folds and curls, instead of being given a reason for their being there. These details say nothing except that the painter is skillful in representing them. We are offered a collection of stage props instead of a message.

There is a fascination in watching any demonstration of acquired skill, which is why tightrope walkers are able to make a living, but unless the skill is directed toward an expressive or productive end it is only diverting. We are diverted by Cot's The Storm; our perception is deepened by Kokoschka's The Tempest. The Cot appeals by telling a little story. It is an anecdote. But the Kokoschka is the emotionalized expression of an idea.

Since we have said nothing favorable about The Storm, why is it included here? Only as a whipping boy? In that case, why is it given exhibition space in one of the greatest museums in the world?

For one thing, it is an absorbing picture to anybody interested in the history of painting because it is a perfect example of the attitude that dominated public taste, and most critical taste too, for half a century. We have said that painting reveals to us what men have thought and felt and believed. If this is important, is it safe to ignore a picture which appealed so strongly to so many people for so long? Museums may set themselves up as arbiters of taste, but they also have a function as visual histories of thought and feeling. We do not exclude important villains and incompetents from our history books just because we don't approve of what they did.

We should ask ourselves, too, why a picture so easy to ridicule is so difficult to dismiss. Right now it seems impossible that serious interest in nineteenth-century academic painting like The Storm can ever revive, but if this should happen, nothing will have happened that has not happened in a similar way to artists as important as El Greco and Botticelli. At this moment there is an enthusiastic renewal of interest in a whole group of sixteenth-century painters who, a few years ago, were regarded with condescension.

If the meaning of a great painting is enriched with time, while that of a poor one withers away, then The Storm is afflicted just now with all the symptoms of being an inferior piece of work. But time is a matter of the very long run. And in the meantime even "bad" paintings are interesting as a counterpoint to the ones we call "good."

What is a painting?

There is no single answer to that question. But whatever else it is, a painting is an experience for the person who looks at it and wants to see. We are ready now to explore some of the areas suggested in this introduction. Our next portfolio is concerned with realism—the world around us as it has been reflected in different ways by painters of different centuries as they have seen it in the light of their times.

Notes on the Painters

James Abbott McNeill Whistler, 1834-1903, American

1. ARRANGEMENT IN GRAY AND BLACK, NO. 1, 1871

Oil on canvas. Height 56". The Louvre Museum, Paris

Whistler, although an American, studied in France and spent his creative years in England under the continuing influence of French painters. His gentle, sensitive art was not a reflection of his public character. He was a dandy, something of an exhibitionist, and a wit. He loved to shock and could cut down an enemy with a phrase or annihilate an aesthetic pretension with an epigram. Such a personality is less out of key with his painting when we know that these fragile, reserved pictures were, in their own way, shockers. They ran against the current of English painting of the day, which was stuffy and sententious. But it is not unusual for a critic to confuse personal and aesthetic values, and Whistler's social arrogance probably accounted as much for the antagonistic reception given his pictures as did the rather mild innovations he introduced in them.

We might add, to what has been said in the body of the text, that Arrangement in Gray and Black owes a great deal to the art of the Japanese print. The flatness of the shapes, the reduction of the background to rectangular areas, the whole conception of composition as the subtle disposition of individually simple forms, is Japanese. Although Whistler was acquainted with Japanese art, the idea of this compositional adaptation came to him through the French impressionists, who were making similar use of it.

Jean Auguste Dominique Ingres, 1780-1867, French

2. MADAME LEBLANC, DATED 1823

Oil on canvas. Height 47". The Metropolitan Museum of Art

Ingres was a pillar—or even a pedant—of the academic tradition in France when the established painters of that neoclassic school were under attack by the new "romantics," whose war cry was for freedom from its arbitrary standards. The term "academic" suggests excessive conservatism and entrenched favoritism. But academic art also has the virtue of insistence on technical proficiency and the preservation of traditional virtues.

Led by Ingres the academicians lost this early battle between traditional and "modern" art. Ingres himself was sometimes guilty of the academic vices, but at his best, as in the portrait of Madame Leblanc, he shows how great a virtue the academic insistence on sound drawing can be. Ingres is one of the great draughtsmen in the history of art. "If a painting is well enough drawn it is well enough painted," he once said. A comparison of Madame Leblanc with the Woman with Chrysanthemums, where color is more freely applied, will show why Ingres's critics call his pictures tinted drawings instead of paintings. Yet Ingres's drawing is not merely imitative of nature. The delight we take in the linear patterns and rhythms in Madame Leblanc comes from their modifications away from the natural appearance of the painted objects, not from their veracity.

Pierre Auguste Renoir, 1841-1919, French

3. MADAME RENOIR, DATED 1884

Oil on canvas. Height 25¾". The Philadelphia Museum of Art, George W. Elkins Collection

4. IN THE MEADOW, ABOUT 1891-92

Oil on canvas. Height 32". The Metropolitan Museum of Art

Renoir was a French leader in the impressionist movement that dominated European painting from about 1863 until the end of the century. This domination, however, is a matter of historical perspective. The young impressionists were obscure and struggling artists who shocked the public by their free use of color, their apparently casual or half-accidental composition, and frequently their subject matter, which ignored the artificial and the ideal in its frank reference to the world as it is.

The most conspicuous names in the impressionist list are Renoir, Degas, Monet, Sisley, and Pissarro. The older painter Manet was a member of the group although he had not developed within it, and the great name of Cézanne must also be included, although he developed in another direction after only a brief impressionist period.

Among these painters Renoir now seems the most traditional. His work can be divided into four periods—the first, in which he was preoccupied with the bright, cheerful effects of light and atmosphere typical of impressionism; the second, when he restudied the old masters, became dissatisfied with the transient effects of impressionism, and painted solid, carefully defined forms; the third, when he tried to combine the virtues of these two periods, returning to the shimmering effects of impressionism while seeking to retain formal solidity; and finally, a fourth period when the intensity of his color and the swollen, rolling character of his forms are an exaggeration of his own style. Madame Renoir belongs to the second period; In the Meadow, to the third.

Hilaire Germain Edgar Degas, 1834-1917, French

5. WOMAN WITH CHRYSANTHEMUMS, DATED 1865

Oil on canvas. Height 29". The Metropolitan Museum of Art

Degas, like Renoir, was a French impressionist. And like Renoir he is much more than a pure impressionist. He is one of the most original and inventive painters of the nineteenth century and one of its great draughtsmen. Because his drawing is not "tight"—which means extremely precise, sharply defined, usually with insistence on detail—the conventional public was at first deceived into thinking it careless. As a matter of fact Degas intensely admired Ingres, the arch-academician and master draughtsman of them all in the most traditional way. Degas's great regret was that he was unable to study under that master. But he is as great a draughtsman as Ingres—his drawing is more flexible while at least as knowledgeable.

Ingres conceived of drawing as a process of reducing nature to an exquisite harmony of line; Degas drew to reveal the truth hidden within a face or a figure. He was fascinated by the chance gestures, the unconsciously assumed attitudes that revealed character and occupation. He set down his observations with the most telling directness and economy. Woman with Chrysanthemums is a brilliant case in point. And in his famous pictures of dancers, it was not the glamour of the ballet that attracted Degas, but the eccentric attitudes of taut, muscular bodies developed by a specialized profession.

Leonardo da Vinci, 1452-1519, Italian

6. MONA LISA, ABOUT 1503

Oil on canvas. Height 30¼". The Louvre Museum, Paris

Leonardo, like his Mona Lisa, is easier to think of as a legend than to recon-
struct as a fact. Living at a time when men still held universal knowledge as
an ideal possible of realization by the individual, Leonardo came as close to
achieving that ideal as any man who ever lived. He was painter, sculptor,
architect, engineer, poet, musician, and scientist. Nothing explains his genius
(he was the illegitimate son of undistinguished parents) and it left little tangible evidence. The paintings he managed to finish have mostly disappeared
or deteriorated beyond repair. His projects in architecture and engineering
remained only that—projects. His inventions and his scientific discoveries
anticipated some of the most important ones of succeeding centuries, but
they were recorded in notes and sketches for only his own satisfaction. They
were unknown to the later scientists and inventors who made practical appli-
cations of the same discoveries. But Leonardo remains, of all men, our symbol of man's capacity for intellectual fulfillment.

His life was as enigmatic as his art. He was a handsome man as well as a
cultured and talented one. His patrons were the great and royal men of the
day. But if he had close personal friends, they appear to have been among
obscure painters of negligible talents. Efforts to create a love affair for him
with one of the several candidates for title of sitter for the Mona Lisa have
produced a great deal of squashy fabrication. Leonardo died in France, in
exile, in the arms—people like to believe—of his then patron, Francis I.

Photo by Giraudon

Asher Brown Durand, 1796-1886, American

7. IMAGINARY LANDSCAPE, DATED 1850

Oil on canvas. Height 39½". The Metropolitan Museum of Art

Durand was one of several American painters grouped under the not
quite accurate title of the Hudson River School. Although these men did
paint views of identified spots in the general area of the Hudson River, their
importance is that they suggested the wildness and mystery of landscape in
imaginative terms even when they painted an existing subject in realistic
detail. Like some others of the group, Durand was an engraver. He had done
little creative painting until, at forty, he discovered landscape. His theories, as
given in advice to his pupils, were naïve, and he apparently liked best in his
work what the public admired most—its hard, rather dry detail. But a painter
is frequently better than his professed theories, sometimes better than his
own idea of what he is doing, and this seems to be the case with Durand in his
Imaginary Landscape.

The grandeur of American landscape was discovered for Durand and
other subsequent members of the Hudson River School by Thomas Cole. A
native of England, where landscape was thoroughly domesticated, Cole was
impressed, as were even earlier European travelers, by the wildness and vastness of a countryside Americans were likely to take for granted. The Hudson
River School maintained close ties with Europe. Durand even took students
there for study. The school's Americanism was spontaneous, rather than cul-
tivated—a healthier state of things than the self-consciousness of much recent
Americanistic art.

Paul Cézanne, 1839-1906, French

8. MONT SAINTE-VICTOIRE, ABOUT 1904

Oil on canvas. Height 27⅞". The Philadelphia Museum of Art

Cézanne, if current evaluations of the Frenchman's art are as valid as they seem, must be thought of with Giotto, the Van Eycks, Michelangelo, and Rembrandt as an initiator of a major shift of direction in the history of painting. Some historians would skip the Van Eycks, Michelangelo, and Rembrandt, contending that Cézanne's is the major revolution in the nearly six hundred years separating him from Giotto. This is because ever since Giotto's discoveries in realistic representation, painters stayed within the bounds of visual credibility no matter how much they modified the appearance of things. But Cézanne abandoned all pretense of reproducing the look of nature. He said he wanted to *re-create* it instead, and he did so by abstracting from it the volumes he wanted, regardless of the consequent deformations of visual reality. He also sought to model in color, rather than in light and shade. These breaks with tradition led directly to the completer abstractions of contemporary painting, with all the complications surrounding us now in midstream of twentieth-century art.

Not every Cézanne you see will conform to these generalities. We have already said (see Renoir, above) that he was for a while associated with impressionism. It is important to remember about Cézanne, too, that although his work grew more and more abstract as he developed his theories, he always held to the conviction that a direct connection between the artist and nature is the vitalizing element in painting. This is the great difference between Cézanne and the contemporary abstractionists who stem from him.

Edward Hicks, 1780-1849, American

9. THE PEACEABLE KINGDOM, ABOUT 1848

Oil on canvas. Height 17⅛". The Philadelphia Museum of Art

Hicks was a Pennsylvania American by birth, a sign painter by trade, a Quaker by religion, and a preacher and artist by avocation. It is impossible to say exactly how many versions of The Peaceable Kingdom he painted or drew. Estimates range around one hundred. It is most likely that he never saw a lion or a leopard. He probably found his models for such exotic animals in children's picture books, among other sources, and he apparently adapted some of his figures of children from poor reproductions of cherubs by Raphael and other renaissance painters.

But whatever Hicks used as source material he transformed by the vigor and precision of his execution and his natural sensitivity to patterns of line and form. Like other good primitive painters he never compromised by sloughing over difficult detail. When he makes a mistake it is a good honest one. It is the combination of explicit realism with poetic fantasy that gives his work its particular flavor, which is no less delightful for being in part the result of his limitations as a self-taught artist.

Jan van Eyck, active by 1422—died 1441, Flemish

10. THE MARRIAGE OF GIOVANNI ARNOLFINI

AND GIOVANNA CENAMI, DATED 1434

Oil on oak. Height 33". The National Gallery, London

Van Eyck and his brother Hubert painted one of the half-dozen decisive landmarks in the history of art, the great altarpiece in the Cathedral Church of St. Bavon in Ghent, Belgium. Historically, their contribution was enormous. They were the first painters to realize the adaptability of oil as a medium to create the flow of light across an object or into a space, and the creation of spatial depth itself. It is not quite true that the Van Eycks invented the oil medium. It was already well known as an adjunct to other techniques. But they developed the oil method to such an extent that it soon replaced the older, more limited ways of working. (Techniques are described in detail in later portfolios.) But the invention of a technique, no matter how important, does not make a painter great. The Van Eycks were great painters because of what they said. They had to develop the technique of oil painting in order to say it.

The explanation of the portrait of Giovanni Arnolfini and Giovanna Cenami is a partial summary of a passage from Erwin Panofsky's *Early Netherlandish Painting*. This work and Dr. Panofsky's great *Dürer* are suggested to any reader interested in a subject barely hinted at here, particularly to any one to whom the idea that works of scholarship may be fascinating reading comes as a surprise.

Pierre Auguste Cot, 1837-1883, French

11. THE STORM, DATED 1880

Oil on canvas. Height 92¼". The Metropolitan Museum of Art

Cot is less important to us as a painter than as a representative example of the academic point of view in France. It is a neat coincidence that he made his debut in the 1863 Salon, which has become notorious for the favoritism and general lack of perception shown by the jury of admission. This was the year of the famous Salon des Refusés, a second exhibition composed of pictures which had been rejected from the official Salon. The Salon des Refusés occupies a position in the history of art analogous to the Declaration of Independence in the history of the United States.

The French Royal Academy of Painting and Sculpture (later the Academy of Fine Arts) was founded under government patronage in 1648. It immediately established its dictatorship in the arts. Running its own art school, doling out government commissions, and giving its members the stamp of approval for important private commissions, the Academy held the power of professional life or death over the artist. Theoretically the Academy's dedication to preserving and cultivating the accumulated knowledge and technique of the past was a great virtue. In practice the preservation of past standards was confused with the stifling of original talent. The resultant dry rot stirred independent painters to a series of revolts in the nineteenth century, culminating in the triumph of impressionism. The Academy has never recovered its prestige.

Oskar Kokoschka, born 1886, Austrian

12. THE TEMPEST, 1914

Oil on canvas. Height 71⅛". Kunstmuseum, Basel

Kokoschka is one of the most enduring painters of the expressionist movement. Expressionism emphasizes emotional content in painting by distortions usually involving dramatically heightened color and emphatic patterns. The term has strong associations with subjects of violence or anguish but need not be so limited in application.

At the end of the nineteenth century the painter Vincent van Gogh was working expressionistically. His art was a source for that of the German, Belgian, Scandinavian, and Austrian painters, including Kokoschka, for whose work the term expressionist was coined. (In a later portfolio we will discuss various forms of expressionism.) Kokoschka's art covers a wide expressive range. The somber and ominous character of our illustration, The Tempest (which has also been called The Wind's Bride), contrasts with other paintings where Kokoschka uses cheerful color applied with great vivacity to express an opposite mood of gaiety and grace. During the Hitler regime Kokoschka was among the many modern painters whose work was outlawed as degenerate. Since expressionist subject matter so frequently deals with poverty, cruelty, and the pathos of human beings degraded through social forces beyond their control, the Nazi objection to expressionist painting was inevitable.